11+ Verbal Activity

CEM Style 20 Minute Tests 1-20

TESTBOOK 1

Dr Stephen C Curran

with Katrina MacKay

Edited by Andrea Richardson

Illustrated by Natalie Knowles

This book belongs to

Ishika

Accelerated Education Publications Ltd.

Verbal Activity Test 1

Read the following passage carefully.

Five siblings moved to the country from London. While playing in a gravel pit they discovered a grumpy sand-fairy, who had the ability to grant one shared wish each day, which would expire at sunset. Their first wish was to be beautiful. The next day:

Anthea woke in the morning from a very real sort of dream, in which she was walking in the Zoological Gardens on a pouring wet day without an umbrella. The animals seemed desperately unhappy because of the rain, and were all growling gloomily. When she awoke, both the growling and the rain went on just the same. The growling was the heavy regular breathing of her sister Jane, who had a slight cold and was still asleep. The rain fell in slow drops on to Anthea's face from the wet corner of a bath-towel out of which her brother Robert was gently squeezing the water, to wake her up, as he now explained. (4)

(8)

"Oh, drop it!" she said rather crossly; so he did, for he was not a brutal brother, though very ingenious in apple-pie beds, booby-traps, original methods of waking sleeping relatives, and the other little accomplishments which make home happy. (12)

"I had such a funny dream," Anthea began.
"So did I," said Jane, waking suddenly and without warning. "I dreamed we found a Sand-fairy in the gravel-pits, and it said it was a nymph, and we might have a new wish every day, and"—— (16)

"But that's what I dreamed," said Robert; "I was just going to tell you,— and we had the first wish directly it said so. And I dreamed you girls were donkeys enough to ask for us all to be beautiful as day, and we jolly well were, and it was perfectly beastly." (20)

An adapted extract from *Five Children and It* by Edith Nesbit (1858-1924).

Glossary
Apple-pie beds (line 10) - the sheets in a bed have been folded in such a way that a person cannot stretch their legs out

Now answer the following questions.

1) How are Jane and Robert related to each other?
   - [ ] a) They are cousins
   - [ ] b) They are brother and sister
   - [ ] c) They are not related
   - [ ] d) They are friends

2) What was the growling noise that Anthea could hear?
   - [ ] a) Her sister breathing
   - [ ] b) The animals making noise
   - [ ] c) Her brother trying to wake her
   - [ ] d) She was snoring

3) What location did Jane dream about?
   - [ ] a) The Zoological Gardens
   - [ ] b) Their house in the country
   - [ ] c) London
   - [ ] d) The gravel-pits

4) What does ingenious (line 10) mean in this context?
   - [ ] a) Foolish
   - [ ] b) Intrusive
   - [ ] c) Inventive
   - [ ] d) Silly

5) Which of the siblings was unwell?
   - [ ] a) Anthea
   - [ ] b) Robert
   - [ ] c) Jane
   - [ ] d) None of them

6) What sort of character lived in the gravel-pits?
   - [ ] a) A donkey
   - [ ] b) A magical creature
   - [ ] c) A beast
   - [ ] d) A newt

7) Why had the children all had the same dream?
   - [ ] a) They had imagined a Sand-fairy had cast a spell on them.
   - [ ] b) They were all told the same bedtime story.
   - [ ] c) They were not fully asleep.
   - [ ] d) In their dreams they were remembering the previous day.

8) How do you think Anthea felt when she awoke?
   - [ ] a) Weary
   - [ ] b) Collected
   - [ ] c) Refreshed
   - [ ] d) Irritated

9) What was Robert's opinion of his sisters' choice of wish?
   - [ ] a) Robert was delighted with their choice.
   - [ ] b) Robert was upset and thought it was a silly idea.
   - [ ] c) Robert wanted to make everybody ugly.
   - [ ] d) Robert was pleased with the outcome of the wish.

10) Robert is described as 'not a brutal brother' (lines 9-10), what does this suggest about his character?
    - [ ] a) He liked to be mean to his sisters.
    - [ ] b) He was just a nasty prankster.
    - [ ] c) His practical jokes were not intended to be harmful.
    - [ ] d) Robert and his sister were not friendly towards each other.

Select the correct words to complete the passage.

There are **11)** [roughly / roguishly / roundly] 1,240 species of bat across the world. Bats are the only mammals that can truly fly, rather than just **12)** [diving / gliding / fleeting]. About 70% of bats **13)** [consume / ate / inhale] insects, the remainder consist of fruit-eating bats; nectar-eating bats; carnivorous bats that **14)** [pry / prey / pray] on small mammals, birds, lizards and frogs; fish-eating bats, and the famous blood-sucking vampire bats of South

America. Bats have 15) [evolve / developed / produced] very 16) [nimble / precision / sensitive] hearing. They 17) [omit / emit / remit] rapid high-pitched squeaks that 18) [shock / contact / bounce] off of objects in their 19) [path / track / lane], echoing back to the bats. From these echoes, the bats can 20) [shape / determine / disprove] the size of objects and how far away they are.

Complete the word on the right so that it means the same as, or nearly the same as, the word on the left.

21) **smart**   i n t e l l i g e n t

22) **exact**   a c c r a t e

23) **sterile**   c l e a n

24) **wrong**   i n c o r r e c t

25) **level**   b a l a n c e d

Score 12   Percentage 48%

Verbal Activity Test 2

Read the following passage carefully.

There is a legend about a heroic rebel called Robin Hood who lived in Sherwood Forest, Nottingham. He and his band of outlaws were skilled archers and swordsmen and robbed from the rich nobles and gave to the poor. The Sheriff of Nottingham was instructed to capture Robin Hood by Prince John. (4) King Richard I, his sibling, was fighting abroad from 1189-1192.

The Sheriff organised a competition to find the finest archer in Nottingham. He believed Robin Hood would attend the event in order to prove his marksmanship. This would give the Sheriff an opportunity to arrest him. Robin (8) Hood's men tried to discourage him from attending as they knew it would be a trap. However, Robin would not listen.

The competition began the next day.
    The Sheriff asked one of his guards, "Is Robin Hood here?" (12)
    He replied, "No, my Lord. Robin Hood has ginger hair and I can't see him."
The Sheriff thought to himself, Robin is too frightened to come.

After ten rounds of the competition, only two competitors were left. The Sheriff's man, William, and another man dressed in green. William shot his (16) last arrow which nearly hit the centre of the target. The crowd applauded enthusiastically. The man in green shot his arrow, it split William's arrow and hit the bull's eye. He then let fly two more arrows in quick succession which landed either side of the Sheriff's chair, narrowly missing his arms. The (20) Sheriff was dumbfounded and furious.

The man in green tore off his black wig and threw it into the cheering crowd.
    The Sheriff yelled, "It's Robin Hood, get after him, you idiots!"
His men gave chase, but Robin Hood leapt over the surrounding wall, jumped (24) onto his horse and galloped away.

An adapted extract from the legends about Robin Hood.

Now answer the following questions.

1) What colour hair did Robin Hood have?
    ☐ a) Black
    ☐ b) Grey
    ☐ c) Blonde
    ☒ d) Red

2) What was unusual about Robin Hood's philosophy?
   - [ ] a) He liked to boast that he was an accurate shot with an arrow.
   - [x] b) He stole from the wealthy and distributed it to the deprived.
   - [ ] c) He enjoyed fighting with swords and shooting arrows.
   - [ ] d) He took from the rich and spent it on himself.

3) How many arrows were fired in the last round?
   - [ ] a) 2
   - [ ] b) 3
   - [x] c) 4
   - [ ] d) 5

4) How did Robin Hood disguise his appearance?
   - [ ] a) He wore a false hairpiece
   - [ ] b) He wore a green outfit
   - [ ] c) He disguised his face
   - [ ] d) He dyed his hair black

5) How many heats were there in the contest?
   - [ ] a) 9
   - [ ] b) 10
   - [x] c) 11
   - [ ] d) 12

6) Why did the Sheriff dislike Robin Hood so much?
   - [ ] a) Robin was the best archer in Nottingham.
   - [ ] b) The Sheriff wanted to be generous to the poor himself.
   - [ ] c) It was no longer safe for the Sheriff to hunt in Sherwood Forest.
   - [x] d) Robin was stealing from the Sheriff's affluent friends.

7) What relation was Prince John to Richard I?
   - [ ] a) His older brother
   - [ ] b) His nephew
   - [x] c) His younger brother
   - [ ] d) His cousin

8) How accurate was Robin's winning arrow?
   - [x] a) It hit the centre of the target.
   - [ ] b) It only just failed to hit the Sheriff.
   - [ ] c) It ricocheted off William's arrow.
   - [ ] d) It was close to the middle of the target.

9) How would you describe Robin's character?
   - [ ] a) He was extremely cautious.
   - [x] b) He was carefree.
   - [ ] c) He was vengeful.
   - [ ] d) He was cowardly.

10) How did the Sheriff feel when Robin escaped?
    - [ ] a) Elated but annoyed
    - [ ] b) Afraid and confused
    - [x] c) Speechless and angry
    - [ ] d) Livid and victorious

Four of the words in each list are linked. Mark the rectangle under the word that is NOT related to these four.

11) teaspoon   plate   fork   knife   spoon

12) trivial   trial   tribal   trail   tribunal

13) doctor   optician   nurse   surgeon   vet

14) injure   hurt   aid   torture   harm

15) bat   bear   buffalo   badger   baboon

Rearrange the words so that each sentence makes sense. Underline the word which does NOT fit into the sentence.

16) same and are I you the can age

17) the see seen you tomorrow library at

18) news quickly the spread speed the throughout town

19) bedrooms has mansion ages eleven the

20) plan mountain to climb that we clime

Choose the word that means the opposite of the word on the left.

21) **friend**	companion	sponsor	foe	comrade
22) **natural**	artificial	organic	relaxed	unprocessed
23) **generous**	charitable	selfish	lavish	subdued
24) **deep**	heartfelt	bass	mysterious	shallow
25) **wealth**	riches	poverty	plethora	plenty

Verbal Activity Test 3

Read the following passage carefully.

Scrooge is a greedy old miser who wants nothing to do with anybody.

Once upon a time—of all the good days in the year, on Christmas Eve—old Scrooge sat busy in his counting-house. It was cold, bleak, biting, foggy weather. He could hear the people in the court outside, go wheezing up and down, beating their hands upon their breasts, and stamping their feet upon the pavement stones to warm them. The city clocks had only just gone three, but it was quite dark already. It had not been light all day and candles were flaring in the windows of the neighbouring offices, like ruddy smears upon the thick brown air. The fog came pouring in at every chink and keyhole, and was so dense, that although the court was of the narrowest, the houses opposite were like phantoms. (4)

(8)

The door of Scrooge's counting-house was open that he might keep his eye upon his clerk, Bob Cratchit, who in a dismal little cell beyond was copying letters. Scrooge had a very small fire, but the clerk's fire was so very much smaller that it looked like one coal. But he couldn't replenish it, for Scrooge kept the coal-box in his own room. As soon as the clerk came in with the shovel, the master made it clear that it would be necessary for him to depart. Wherefore the clerk put on his white comforter, and tried to warm himself at the candle; in which effort, not being a man of a strong imagination, he failed. (12)

(16)

"A merry Christmas, uncle! God save you!" *cried a cheerful voice. It was the voice of Scrooge's nephew, who came upon him so quickly that this was the first indication he had of his approach.* (20)

"Bah!" *said Scrooge,* "Humbug!"

An adapted extract from *A Christmas Carol* by Charles Dickens (1812-1870).

<u>Glossary</u>
Miser – a person who spends as little money as possible

Now answer the following questions.

1) At what time of day is this passage set?
   - [ ] a) Midday
   - [x] b) 3pm
   - [ ] c) Twilight
   - [ ] d) 3am

2) Where does the story take place?
    - [ ] a) A village
    - [ ] b) The countryside
    - [x] c) A large town
    - [ ] d) A hamlet

3) What was the mood of Scrooge's nephew?
    - [ ] a) Serious
    - [ ] b) Frosty
    - [ ] c) Hopeful
    - [x] d) Jolly

4) What was the clerk not allowed to do?
    - [ ] a) Collect more coal for his fire
    - [ ] b) Light another candle
    - [x] c) Go home early
    - [ ] d) Count money

5) What was the visibility like?
    - [ ] a) Clear
    - [x] b) Murky
    - [ ] c) Stormy
    - [ ] d) Moonlit

6) How would you describe Scrooge's character?
    - [ ] a) Considerate
    - [x] b) Violent
    - [ ] c) Stingy
    - [ ] d) Charitable

7) What do you think 'comforter' (line 17) means?
    - [ ] a) Boots
    - [ ] b) Reading glasses
    - [ ] c) Wig
    - [x] d) Scarf

8) What was Scrooge's attitude towards Bob Cratchit?
   - [x] a) Suspicious
   - [ ] b) Trusting
   - [ ] c) Jealous
   - [ ] d) Kindly

9) Why were people wheezing (line 3)?
   - [ ] a) People were out of breath.
   - [ ] b) The air was polluted.
   - [ ] c) It was very humid.
   - [x] d) People had colds.

10) Why does Scrooge say, 'Bah! Humbug!' (line 22)?
    - [ ] a) He does not like his nephew.
    - [x] b) He does not like being disturbed at work.
    - [ ] c) The cold weather makes him irritable.
    - [ ] d) He does not believe in the meaning of Christmas.

> Fill in the missing letters to complete the passage.

Submarines are a form of 11) `v e t s l e` that can operate underwater.

They are typically large 12) `_ t r _ c _ u r _ s` with a big

crew; a 13) `n _ c l _ _ r` submarine can have a crew of over 100

people. Submarines serve many purposes, but their main use is in the

14) `m i l i t a r y` forming part of the 15) `c a v e`. They

are required to perform 16) `o b s e r v a t i o n` missions and

protect aircraft 17) `c a _ r _ _ r s`, amongst other tasks.

Submarines use ballast tanks to hold water, this allows them to submerge and

18) | e | | | r | | e | as necessary. Some have the ability to

19) | r | e | | | | n | submerged for months at a time. Most submarines

feature a raised tower which holds radar 20) | | q | u | i | | m | | | t | and

the periscope.

> Choose the word that means the same as the word on the left.

21) **panic**   security   **fright**   basic   calm

22) **brief**   lengthy   **mild**   vast   hasty

23) **familiar**   **common**   thick   unusual   foreign

24) **mute**   vocal   free   **muffle**   raise

25) **sole**   only   mixed   **not**   mutual

Score 11 Percentage 44%

Verbal Activity Test 4

> Read the following passage carefully.

President Lincoln, who led the Union armies to victory in the American Civil War (1861-1865), was shot in the right-hand side of the back of his head on the 14th April 1865 while at the theatre. His assassin was John Wilkes Booth, a Confederate sympathiser, who disagreed with his army's surrender on 9th April 1865. Lincoln was treated by Doctor Hall at a local house. Gideon Welles, who served as Lincoln's Naval Secretary, documents the events that followed.

"The giant sufferer lay extended diagonally across the bed, which was not long enough for him. He had been stripped of his clothes. His large arms, which were occasionally exposed, were of a size which one would scarce have expected from his appearance. His slow, full respiration lifted the clothes with (4) each breath that he took. His features were calm and striking. I had never seen them appear to better advantage than for the first hour, perhaps, that I was there. After that his right eye began to swell and that part of his face became discoloured. (8)

The room was small and overcrowded. About once an hour through the night Mrs. Lincoln would repair to the bedside of her dying husband and with lamentation and tears remain until overcome by emotion.

A little before seven I went into the room where the dying President was (12) *rapidly drawing near the closing moments. Soon after, his wife made her last visit to him. The death struggle had begun. Robert, his son, stood with several others at the head of the bed. He bore himself well but on two occasions gave way to overpowering grief and sobbed aloud. The respiration of the President* (16) *became suspended at intervals and at last entirely ceased at twenty-two minutes past seven."*

An adapted extract from *Diary of Gideon Welles, Secretary of the Navy under Lincoln and Johnson* by Gideon Welles (1802-1878).

Glossary
Lamentation (line 11) – the expression of grief or sorrow
Union – those who wanted to keep the USA as
     one country
Confederate – those who want to set up an independent
     country alongside the USA

> Now answer the questions on the following pages.

1) At what time did the President die?
   - [x] a) 7.22pm
   - [ ] b) 7.22am
   - [ ] c) Just before seven
   - [ ] d) 6.38am

2) What was Lincoln doing when he was shot?
   - [ ] a) Giving a speech.
   - [ ] b) Dining at home with his family.
   - [x] c) Watching a play.
   - [ ] d) Sleeping in his bed.

3) Why did Lincoln's right eye swell?
   - [ ] a) He hit his head when he fell.
   - [ ] b) The bullet hit him in the eye.
   - [ ] c) He had lost his vision in that eye.
   - [x] d) The location of the bullet.

4) How did the president breathe at first?
   - [ ] a) Deep, steady breaths
   - [ ] b) Rapid, intermittent breaths
   - [ ] c) Slow, shallow breaths
   - [x] d) Rasping, desperate breaths

5) What expression did Lincoln have on his face to begin with?
   - [x] a) Distressed
   - [ ] b) Blank
   - [ ] c) Composed
   - [ ] d) Anguished

6) How long after the fighting had stopped was it before Lincoln was shot?
   - [ ] a) 3 days
   - [ ] b) 4 days
   - [ ] c) 5 days
   - [x] d) 1 month

7) Why did Mrs Lincoln leave her husband's bedside?
   - [ ] a) To comfort her son.
   - [x] b) She had feelings of grief.
   - [ ] c) She was embarrassed about being upset before others.
   - [ ] d) She felt helpless and the room was overcrowded.

8) What is meant by 'the death struggle' (line 14)?
   - [ ] a) He had given up the will to live
   - [ ] b) The doctor's attempts to save him
   - [ ] c) He became conscious before death
   - [x] d) The final minutes of life

9) Why was Lincoln's assassination so tragic?
   - [ ] a) He had only just won the Civil War
   - [ ] b) He had a family
   - [ ] c) He was a much loved president
   - [ ] d) He was assassinated by a loyal supporter

10) How did Lincoln's son behave at the bedside?
    - [ ] a) He cried continually
    - [x] b) He was courageous but broke down
    - [ ] c) He wanted to leave immediately
    - [ ] d) He was controlled and only wept once

Complete the word on the right so that it means the opposite of the word on the left.

11) **wide** — n a r r o w

12) **ancient** — m o d e r n

13) **full** — e m p t y

14) **courageous** — c o w a r d l y

15) **arrival** — d e p a r t u r e

Choose the word that has a similar meaning to the words in both sets of brackets.

16) (twig, branch) (push, insert)   pull   tree   division   stick   stem ✓

17) (calculate, tally) (nobleman, earl)   count   score   king   lord   gauge ✓

18) (strength, power) (possibly, shall)   control   perhaps   force   maybe   might ✗

19) (joy, delight) (arrogance, vanity)   bliss   pride   wonder   haughty   self ✗

20) (fragment, piece) (quarrel, row)   part   tiff   scrap   argument   slice ✓

Four of the words in each list are linked. Mark the rectangle under the word that is NOT related to these four.

21) sad   elated   sorry   dismal   unhappy ✓

22) chameleon   whale   shark   eel   seal ✓

23) jumping   skipping   hoping   running   leaping ✗

24) college   university   nursery   office   school ✗

25) true   bamboo   yew   flu   catalogue ✓

Score 15   Percentage 60 %

Verbal Activity Test 5

> Read the following passage carefully.

Tom Sawyer grew up along the Mississippi River, USA, in the 1840s.

Tom found the summer evenings were long. Night was drawing in. Suddenly a stranger was before him—a boy a shade larger than himself. A newcomer of any age was an impressive curiosity in the poor little shabby village of St. Petersburg. This boy was well dressed and it was not even Sunday. This was simply astounding. His cap was a dainty thing, his close-buttoned blue cloth jacket was new and natty, and so were his trousers. He even had shoes on and wore a bright ribbon necktie. He had a refined air about him that irritated Tom. As Tom stared at the splendid marvel, the more he turned up his nose at the boy's fine clothes and the shabbier and shabbier his own outfit felt. Neither boy spoke. If one moved, the other moved—but only sidewise, in a circle; they kept face to face and eye to eye all the time. (4) (8)

   Finally Tom said, "I can lick you!" (12)
   "I'd like to see you try it."

In an instant both boys were rolling and tumbling in the dirt, gripped together like cats; and for a minute they tugged and tore at each other's hair and clothes, punched and scratched each other's nose, and covered themselves with dust and glory. Presently the confusion took form, and through the fog of battle Tom appeared, seated astride the new boy, and pounding him with his fists. (16)

   "Enough?" (20)
The boy only struggled to free himself. He was crying—mainly from rage.
   "Had enough?"—and the pounding went on.
   At last the stranger got out a smothered, "Enough!"
   Tom let him up and said, "Now that'll learn you. Better look out who you're fooling with next time." (24)

An adapted extract from *The Adventures of Tom Sawyer* by Mark Twain (1835-1910).

> Now answer the following questions.

1) In which century did this story take place?
   - [ ] a) 17th century
   - [ ] b) 18th century
   - [x] c) 19th century
   - [ ] d) 20th century

2) How would you describe the newcomer's appearance?
   - [x] a) Formal
   - [ ] b) Scruffy
   - [ ] c) Casual
   - [ ] d) Ill-fitting

3) At what time of day did this event occur?
   - [ ] a) Night-time
   - [ ] b) Afternoon
   - [ ] c) Day-time
   - [ ] d) Dusk

4) What is meant by 'refined air' (line 7)?
   - [ ] a) Rough and ready
   - [x] b) Cultured and sophisticated
   - [ ] c) Friendly and approachable
   - [ ] d) Proud and stern

5) What happened when the two boys first met?
   - [ ] a) They conversed.
   - [ ] b) They struggled to make eye contact.
   - [ ] c) The newcomer backed away.
   - [x] d) There was a standoff.

6) Why would Tom not give way to the boy?
   - [ ] a) The village was his territory.
   - [ ] b) The boy was bigger than Tom.
   - [ ] c) He saw the boy at church on Sunday.
   - [ ] d) The boy wanted to befriend Tom.

7) How did Tom feel about the newcomer's clothes?
   - [ ] a) He was indecisive.
   - [x] b) He was self-conscious.
   - [ ] c) He was nervous.
   - [ ] d) He was indifferent.

8) How did the boy's demeanour affect Tom?
   - [ ] a) He felt proud of being shoddy.
   - [ ] b) He felt superior.
   - [x] c) He felt inferior.
   - [ ] d) He felt confident.

9) How would you describe Tom's character?
   - [x] a) Tough and coarse
   - [ ] b) Mannered and cultivated
   - [ ] c) Cowardly and timid
   - [ ] d) Fair and reasonable

10) How was the fight resolved?
    - [ ] a) The boys stopped due to exhaustion.
    - [ ] b) The newcomer started crying.
    - [ ] c) Both boys were scratched and bleeding.
    - [x] d) The newcomer surrendered.

Choose the correct words from the word bank to complete the passage.

A exceeded	B realms	C monarch	D prime	E state
F status	G reign	H milestone	I history	J throne

On Wednesday 9th September 2015, the 23,226th day of her **11)** _reign_,

Queen Elizabeth II became the longest reigning **12)** _monarch_ of the

United Kingdom. Her reign of 63 years and seven months **13)** _exceeded_

the record set by her great-great-grandmother Queen Victoria. Queen Elizabeth

came to the **14)** _____ at the age of 25 and her reign has included 12

different **15)** _Prime_ ministers. She is Head of the Commonwealth and sovereign of 15 Commonwealth 16) _____ alongside the UK; a head of 17) _____ for 138 million people. This 18) _____ also marks Elizabeth II's 19) _____ as the longest reigning female monarch in world 20) _____.

> Rearrange the words so that each sentence makes sense. Underline the word which does NOT fit into the sentence.

21) wait not further notice please until

22) unreliable timekeeping was can his

23) the it was disappointing were for a result team

24) and can speak an English French he both

25) had a sense of tense direction bad she

Verbal Activity Test 6

> Read the following passage carefully.

It was claimed the Titanic was the safest ship ever constructed. The ship's designers believed she was so safe, she only had 20 lifeboats, which were only intended to rescue survivors from other ships that had foundered. They believed the Titanic was 'unsinkable'.

The maiden voyage of the White Star liner Titanic, the largest ship ever launched, has ended in disaster.

The Titanic started her trip from Southampton for New York on Wednesday. Late on the following Sunday night she struck an iceberg at 11.40pm off the Grand Banks of Newfoundland. By wireless telegraphy she sent out signals of distress, and several liners were near enough to respond to the call. Conflicting news, alarming and reassuring, was current yesterday. Even after midnight it was said all the passengers were safe. All reports, of course, depend on wireless telegrams over great distances. (4)
(8)

Late last night the White Star officials in New York announced that a message had been received stating that the Titanic sank at 02:20 that morning after all her passengers and crew had been transferred to another vessel. The main hope that remains is that other vessels may have picked up more of the passengers and crew than those saved by the liner Carpathia. As to this there is no news at the time of writing. (12)

The White Star official, Mr Franklin said, "I was confident today when I made the statement that the Titanic was unsinkable that the steamship was safe and that there would be no loss of life." (16)

The first definite news to the contrary came in a later message. The White Star officials eventually admitted that probably only 675 out of 2,200 passengers on board the Titanic had been saved. (20)

'The Titanic is sunk, with great loss of life', *The Guardian*, Tuesday 16th April 1912.

> Now answer the following questions.

1) On what date did the Titanic start her trip?
   - [ ] a) 9th April 1912
   - [x] b) 10th April 1912
   - [ ] c) 11th April 1912
   - [ ] d) 12th April 1912

2) Did the Titanic have enough lifeboats?
   - [ ] a) Too many
   - [ ] b) More than enough
   - [ ] c) Just enough
   - [x] d) Not enough

3) How long did it take the Titanic to sink?
   - [x] a) 2 hours 40 minutes
   - [ ] b) 26 hours 40 minutes
   - [ ] c) 1 hour 20 minutes
   - [ ] d) 2 hours 20 minutes

4) Why were people so confident that the Titanic was a safe ship?
   - [ ] a) She could communicate with wireless telegraphy.
   - [x] b) They thought it was unsinkable.
   - [ ] c) Her hull was made from reinforced steel.
   - [ ] d) She was a large and fast ship.

5) What ship assisted the stranded passengers?
   - [ ] a) The Olympia
   - [x] b) The White Star
   - [ ] c) The Carpathia Line 14
   - [ ] d) The Grand Banks

6) Why did early news reports about the Titanic disagree?
   - [ ] a) Messages were carried across vast expanses.
   - [x] b) The ship's owners withheld information.
   - [ ] c) The wireless did not work.
   - [ ] d) Vessels in the area gave false information.

7) Where did the Titanic strike the iceberg?
   - [x] a) Southampton docks
   - [ ] b) The Horn of Africa
   - [ ] c) Off the coast of Canada   Newfoundand = Canadian coast
   - [ ] d) New York harbour

8) What is meant by the phrase 'maiden voyage' (line 1)?
- [x] a) It was the Titanic's last crossing.
- [ ] b) The Titanic was named after a medieval woman.
- [x] c) It was the Titanic's first sailing.
- [ ] d) It was the first ship built by the White Star Line.

9) What proportion of the passengers were eventually thought to have been saved?
- [ ] a) More than a quarter
- [ ] b) Over a half
- [x] c) Less than a quarter
- [ ] d) Nearly a third

10) How do you think Mr Franklin is likely to have felt upon receiving the truth about the Titanic?
- [x] a) Blameless and detached
- [ ] b) Hopeful and optimistic
- [x] c) Embarrassed and guilty
- [ ] d) Assured and defiant

Choose the word that has a similar meaning to the words in both sets of brackets.

11) (armour, exterior) shield   mine   shell   strike   external
    (attack, bomb)

12) (mother, parent)   figure   paternal   cadaver   parental   mummy
    (corpse, body)

13) (single, solitary)   sole   maroon   lone   marine   solo
    (cod, plaice)

14) (hint, pinch)   clue   lock   touch   dash   tweak
    (dart, bolt)

15) (wellington, wader)   pump   boot   punt   foot   spur
    (kick, drive)

Complete the word on the right so that it means the same as, or nearly the same as, the word on the left.

16) **able** — c o m p e t e n t

17) **mistrustful** — s u s p i c i o u s

18) **fair** — f e s t i v a l

19) **malevolent** — v e n g e f u l

20) **accommodating** — o b l i g i n g

Choose the word that means the opposite of the word on the left.

21) **mistakenly** — error / correctly / misguidedly / respectably

22) **meritorious** — laudable / exemplary / benefit / dishonourable

23) **intuitive** — calculated / innate / sense / untaught

24) **sour** — acidic / rancid / sweet / nasty

25) **unrefined** — crude / cultured / coarse / crass

Score ___ Percentage ___ %

Verbal Activity Test 7

> Read the following passage carefully.

A shepherd boy tended his master's sheep near a dark forest, not far from the village. Soon he found life in the pasture very dull. All he could do to amuse himself was to <u>talk to his dog</u> or <u>play on his shepherd's pipe.</u>

One day, as he sat watching the sheep and the quiet forest, and thinking what he would do should he see a wolf, he thought of a plan to amuse himself. His master had told him to call for help should a wolf attack the flock, and the villagers would drive it away. (4)

So now, though he had not seen anything that even looked like a wolf, he ran toward the village shouting at the top of his voice, "Wolf! Wolf!" As he expected, the villagers who heard the cry dropped their work and ran in great excitement to the pasture. But when they got there they found the boy doubled up with laughter at the trick he had played on them. (8)

(12)

A few days later the shepherd boy again yelled, "Wolf! Wolf!" Again the villagers ran to help him, only to be laughed at again. Then one <u>evening as the sun was setting</u> behind the forest and the shadows were creeping out over the pasture, a wolf really did spring from the underbrush and fall upon the sheep. (16)

In terror the boy ran toward the village screaming, "Wolf! Wolf!" Although the villagers heard the cry, they did not run to help him as they had before. (20)

"He cannot fool us again," they said.
The wolf killed a great many of the boy's sheep and after eating the boy, slipped away into the forest.

'The Shepherd Boy and the Wolf' from *The Aesop for Children* (1919).

> Now answer the following questions.

1) How many times did the boy play a trick on the villagers?
   - [ ] a) Once
   - [✓] b) Twice
   - [■] c) Three times
   - [ ] d) Multiple times

© 2015 Stephen Curran

2) Why did the villagers ignore the boy when the wolf attacked?
   - [ ] a) Wolves did not regularly attack sheep.
   - [x] b) They did not care for the boy's safety.
   - [ ] c) Boys were less trustworthy than girls.
   - [ ] d) The boy had lost their trust.

3) Which of the following did the boy not do to pass the time?
   - [ ] a) Speak to his dog
   - [ ] b) Trick the villagers
   - [x] c) Seek out the wolf
   - [ ] d) Play a musical instrument

4) What is the moral of this story?
   - [ ] a) Liars are not believed even when they speak the truth.
   - [ ] b) Some people do not believe you even when you speak the truth.
   - [x] c) Jokes do not usually backfire on us.
   - [ ] d) It is alright to lie providing it does not hurt people.

5) How did the boy feel about his life as a shepherd?
   - [ ] a) He was interested in his work.
   - [x] b) He found it tiresome.
   - [ ] c) He cared about the sheep.
   - [ ] d) He enjoyed being alone.

6) If a wolf came, how were the villagers expected to help?
   - [ ] a) Chase off the wolf
   - [ ] b) Take the boy to safety
   - [ ] c) Round up the sheep
   - [x] d) Shoot the wolf

7) Why did the boy find his pranks so funny?
   - [ ] a) The villagers could have been eaten by the wolf.
   - [ ] b) He enjoyed the villagers' company.
   - [x] c) He had made everybody look like a fool.
   - [ ] d) He was practising for a real attack.

8) Why is this story a tragedy?
- [ ] a) The master had to employ another boy.
- [x] b) The boy lost his life.
- [ ] c) All the sheep died.
- [ ] d) The villagers wasted a lot of time.

9) At what time of day did the wolf attack?
- [x] a) Dusk
- [ ] b) Midnight
- [x] c) Noon
- [ ] d) Dead of night

10) How did the villagers' feel about the boy's tricks?
- [ ] a) Amused
- [ ] b) Excited
- [ ] c) Sympathetic
- [x] d) Irritated

Select the correct words to complete the passage.

Lunar craters are large, bowl-shaped 11) [ ] opening / [ ] cavities / [x] disks on the surface of Earth's Moon. The Moon's crust has many craters formed as a result of 12) [ ] pileups / [ ] retractions / [x] collisions with asteroids, meteorites, and other space 13) [ ] debris / [ ] discus / [x] drifts, over the past few billion years. The Earth has less craters than the Moon because it is 14) [x] surrounded / [ ] covering / [ ] layered by an atmosphere which 15) [ ] forms / [x] causes / [ ] made asteroids to burn up before they can reach the surface. The Moon's **16)** ☒ lack / ☐ lax / ☐ lac of atmosphere means there is no wind or rain, and hence no **17)** ☒ evasion / ☐ ovation / ☐ erosion, therefore the craters stay there **18)** ☒ permanently / ☐ temporarily / ☐ sometimes. In contrast, the Earth's craters are often **19)** ☐ detrimental / ☒ deteriorated / ☐ determine by these forces. The largest lunar crater recorded is about 181 miles in **20)** ☐ decimetre / ☐ decilitre / ☒ diameter.

Complete the word on the right so that it means the **opposite** of the word on the left.

21)	experienced	n	a	e	i	v	e	(novice)
22)	remarkable	c	o	m	m	o	n	p	l	a	c	e
23)	distracted	a	t	t	e	n	t	i	v	e
24)	invisible	d	e	t	e	c	t	a	b	l	e
25)	reprimand	c	o	m	m	e	n	d

Score 13   Percentage 52%

Verbal Activity Test 8

Read the following passage carefully.

Valentine was a priest in Rome during the reign of Emperor Claudius II (268-270 CE). A legend claims he was accused of marrying soldiers in a Christian ceremony, who were forbidden to wed during their military service. Valentine was tried by the Prefect of Rome, then clubbed to death and beheaded. While awaiting execution, he allegedly healed his jailer's daughter, Asterius, and wrote her a final letter signed, 'Your Valentine.' Valentine was martyred on 14th February 269 CE during the ancient spring festival, called Lupercalia. This festival was dedicated to the gods and held from 13th to 15th of February. (4) (8)

The early Christian Church replaced the Roman festival with one dedicated to the memory of Valentine and his loving acts. Saint Valentine's Day was first declared on 14th February 496 CE by Pope Galasius. Since then, many customs have developed linking this festival to romantic love. For example, if a man was drawn to a particular woman he might pin a heart-shaped piece of paper on his sleeve bearing the lady's name. This is the origin of the saying, 'wearing your heart on your sleeve'. A woman might show who she liked by wearing a charm around her neck. This is mentioned in Samuel Pepys' diary on 3rd March 1662, when a lady friend of his displays his name on a necklace she is wearing, saying he is her valentine. Another custom, in the 18th century, involved the names of young women being placed in a box. Men would draw out a name by chance and the girl would be called their valentine. This was seen as a prediction that, one day, they might marry. (12) (16) (20)

Today, Valentine's Day is celebrated on 14th February and people send anonymous cards to each other declaring their love.

Now answer the following questions.

1) How was Valentine killed?
   - [ ] a) Crucified
   - [ ] b) Decapitated
   - [ ] c) Beaten until dead
   - [x] d) Beheaded

2) What does 'martyred' (line 6) mean?
   - [x] a) Dying for your beliefs
   - [ ] b) Acting in a loving way
   - [ ] c) Being willing to die for someone else
   - [ ] d) Having a celebration named after you

3) After his death, how long did the church take to recognise Valentine?
   - [ ] a) 1,393 years
   - [ ] b) 227 years
   - [x] c) 1,662 years
   - [ ] d) 226 years

4) Who recalls an important Valentine's tradition in his writings?
   - [ ] a) Emperor Claudius II
   - [x] b) Asterius
   - [ ] c) Pope Galasius
   - [ ] d) Samuel Pepys

5) What do you think is the significance of Valentine's Day in modern times?
   - [ ] a) An opportunity to receive cards
   - [x] b) A way to secretly show our affections
   - [ ] c) A chance to dress up
   - [ ] d) A way to trick people into liking us

6) What do you think 'wearing your heart on your sleeve' (line 15) really means?
   - [x] a) Concealing your feelings
   - [ ] b) Wearing a heart shaped badge
   - [ ] c) Expressing your emotions openly
   - [ ] d) Making a marriage proposal

7) How did men find their Valentine three centuries ago?
   - [ ] a) By luck
   - [x] b) Choosing someone they liked
   - [ ] c) By parental arrangement
   - [ ] d) Through recommendation

8) Where does the tradition of being someone's 'Valentine' come from?
- ■ a) The Lupercalia festival
- ☐ b) Wearing a charm
- ☐ c) The announcement from Pope Galasius
- ☐ d) Valentine's letter to Asterius

9) Why was Valentine executed?
- ■ a) He was a Christian priest.
- ☐ b) He fell in love with Asterius.
- ☐ c) He was breaking Roman law.
- ☐ d) He refused to celebrate the spring festival.

10) What well-known symbol is used today to symbolise love?
- ☐ a) A necklace
- ■ b) A heart
- ☐ c) Jewellery
- ☐ d) A card

> Choose the word that means the same as the word on the left.

11) **lax** — strict ■ | slack ☐ | severe ☐ | sharp ☐

12) **jealous** — trusting ☐ | sceptical ☐ | naïve ☐ | envious ■

13) **article** — disagree ☐ | oppose ☐ | object ■ | protest ☐

14) **nascent** — budding ☐ | smell ☐ | dying ☐ | aroma ■

15) **epidemic** — native ■ | illness ☐ | plague ☐ | vaccine ☐

Four of the words in each list are linked. Mark the rectangle under the word that is NOT related to these four.

16) copper   tin ▨   plastic   lead   iron

17) scene   disciple   ascended   crescent   scalded ▨

18) scorch   singe   char ▨   stifle   brand

19) moan ▨   one ✗   sown   phone   disown

20) variant ▨   matching   identical   alike   duplicate ✗

Complete the word on the right so that it means the opposite of the word on the left.

21) **unattached**   j | o | i | n | e | d

22) **plain**   d | e | c | o | r | a | t | i | d | e

23) **resolute**   h | o | s | s | t | a | n | e

24) **civil**   f | o | r | e | i | g | n

25) **undeveloped**   _ | a | t | _ | r

Score ☐   Percentage ☐ %

Verbal Activity Test 9

Read the following passage carefully.

There was once a little girl who was very wilful and never obeyed her elders.
*   One day she said to her parents, "I have heard so much of the old witch that I will go and see her. People say she is a wonderful old woman, and has many marvellous things in her house, and I am very curious to see them."* (4)
*   Her parents forbade her, "The witch is a wicked old woman, who performs many evil deeds. If you go near her, you are no longer a child of ours." The girl, however, would not listen and went to the witch's house.*

*   When she arrived there the old woman asked her, "Why are you so pale?"* (8)
*   "Ah," she replied, trembling all over, "I have frightened myself so with what I have just seen."*
*   "And what did you see?" inquired the old witch.*
*   "I saw a man dressed in black on your steps."* (12)
*   "That was a collier," she replied.*
*   "Then I saw a man in a grey tweed blazer."*
*   "That was a hunter," said the old woman.*
*   "After him I saw a man with blood on his clothes."* (16)
*   "That was a butcher," replied the witch.*
*   "But I was most terrified," continued the girl, "when I peeped through your window, and saw not you, but a creature with a fiery head."*
*   "Then you have seen the witch in her proper dress," said the old woman.* (20) *"For you I have long waited, and now you shall give me light."*
*   So saying the witch changed the little girl into a block of wood, threw it on the fire and sat down on the hearth warming herself, "How good I feel! The fire has not burned like this for a long time!"* (24)

Adapted from *The Old Witch* by the Brothers Grimm who lived from 1785–1863.

Notes on Text:
Collier (line 13) – a coal miner
Fiery (line 19) – burning or scorching

Now answer the following questions.

1) What does the word wilful (line 1) mean?
 ☐ a) Willing
 ☐ b) Obstinate
 ☐ c) Respectful
 ▨ d) Naughty ✗

34   © 2015 Stephen Curran

2) What did the parents threaten to do should the girl visit the witch?
- [x] a) Disown her
- [ ] b) Forbid her to go out
- [ ] c) Beat her
- [ ] d) Accompany her to see the witch

3) What do you think the moral of the story is?
- [ ] a) Stay away from evil witches.
- [ ] b) Curiosity is educational.
- [x] c) Listen to the advice of your elders.
- [ ] d) Do not talk to strangers.

4) Where did the man dressed in black work?
- [ ] a) In an ironworks
- [ ] b) In a blacksmith's forge
- [ ] c) In a quarry
- [x] d) In a coal mine

5) What happened to the girl at the end of the story?
- [x] a) She died in the fireplace.
- [ ] b) She escaped as a block of wood.
- [ ] c) She turned the witch into timber.
- [ ] d) She died in the oven.

6) Why did the colour drain from the little girl's face?
- [ ] a) She felt ill.
- [ ] b) She was shocked.
- [x] c) She was cold.
- [ ] d) She was scared.

7) What was the true appearance of the witch?
- [x] a) An ugly old woman
- [ ] b) A being with a flaming scalp
- [ ] c) A fire-breathing dragon
- [ ] d) A creature with burning scales

8) Why did the girl want to visit the witch?
- [ ] a) She knew the witch would approve of her disobedience.
- [ ] b) She hoped the witch would give her presents.
- [x] c) She was intrigued by the rumours about the witch.
- [ ] d) She wanted to learn magic spells.

9) What item of clothing is mentioned in the passage?
- [x] a) A cloak
- [ ] b) A jacket
- [ ] c) An overcoat
- [ ] d) A cape

10) Why might the last two men seem scarier to the girl than the first?
- [ ] a) They killed things.
- [ ] b) They were both cruel.
- [x] c) She saw blood on them.
- [ ] d) They both worked for the witch.

Fill in the missing letters to complete the passage.

The 11) c o _ _ a c _ team sport of rugby union

12) o _ i _ i n _ t e _ at Rugby School, England, in the 19th century. It is played by two teams of fifteen players using an oval-shaped ball

on a 13) r e _ _ a n _ _ l _ r field with H-shaped

14) _ o a _ p _ _ t s. Players can run while holding the ball,

kick it and pass it, but 15) p a s s i n g forwards is

16) f o r b i d e n n. Players can tackle an

17) _ p _ _ n _ n t in order to 18) o b _ _ i _ the ball.

There are **19)** | s | e | | r | | l | ways to score points, including a try (five points), a conversion (two points) and a goal kick (three points). Rugby union is played in over 100 countries **20)** | | c | r | | | s | six continents.

> Rearrange the words so that each sentence makes sense. Underline the word which does NOT fit into the sentence.

21) is at deepest the <u>waters</u> lake this point

22) I know camera do <u>shot</u> not to use how this

23) <u>can</u> mail the lost in the got postcard

24) for my <u>a</u> I present looking mother for am search

25) <u>in</u> train twenty the by journey minutes takes

Score 11 Percentage 44%

Verbal Activity Test 10

Read the following passage carefully.

Anne Frank was born in 1929 in Germany. When the Nazis took power in 1933 and began to persecute the Jews, the Frank family fled to Amsterdam. In 1940 the Germans invaded the Netherlands, and on 5th July 1942 Anne's sister, Margot, was commanded to report to a Nazi work camp. The family (4) went into hiding the next day in concealed rooms at the back of their father Otto's workplace. The entrance to the 'Secret Annexe' was hidden behind a bookcase in Otto's former office, which was still in use. During the day, the family had to remain silent to prevent detection. (8)

To pass the time, Anne wrote secretly in a diary she had received on her thirteenth birthday. She addressed her daily entries to Kitty, her imaginary friend. The first entry read, "I hope I will be able to confide everything to you and you will be a great source of comfort and support." The family spent two (12) years in hiding, never going outside, receiving provisions from trusted friends. This was demanding and Anne wrote on 3rd February 1944, "I've reached the point where I hardly care whether I live or die."

They were given away by an anonymous betrayer and on 4th August 1944 (16) the Nazis stormed the apartment. Anne and her sister were transported to Auschwitz concentration camp in Poland where they were made to haul heavy stones. Eventually they were moved to Bergen-Belsen concentration camp in Germany, where food was scarce and they contracted typhus. Both sisters (20) died a few weeks before the British soldiers liberated the camp in March 1945. Otto, the family's only surviving member, published her diary in 1952.

Anne was just one of over a million Jewish children who died during the Holocaust. (24)

Now answer the following questions.

1) What country did the family escape to?
   - a) Germany
   - b) Holland
   - c) Belgium
   - ☒ d) Poland

2) For how long were the family in hiding?
   - [ ] a) 7 months
   - [x] b) 2 years and 1 month
   - [ ] c) 26 months
   - [ ] d) 1 year 7 months

3) Which of the following ultimately caused Anne's death?
   - [ ] a) Hard labour
   - [ ] b) Starvation
   - [x] c) Disease
   - [ ] d) Torture

4) What caused the family to move to the secret apartment?
   - [x] a) The Nazi's invaded Amsterdam.
   - [ ] b) The Jews were being victimised.
   - [ ] c) The Nazi party took control of the government.
   - [ ] d) Margot was being forced to work for the Germans.

5) What do Anne's writings reveal about how she felt after being in hiding for a long period?
   - [ ] a) Depressed
   - [ ] b) Hopeful
   - [x] c) Consoled
   - [ ] d) Fearful

6) Why was it dangerous to make noise during the day in the annexe?
   - [x] a) Otto needed to sleep during the day.
   - [ ] b) Spies suspected they were living there.
   - [ ] c) The bookcase might not be soundproof.
   - [ ] d) The business was still in operation.

7) What was significant about the informer?
   - [x] a) It was a personal friend.
   - [ ] b) It was someone who probably knew the family.
   - [ ] c) It was later revealed to be a work colleague.
   - [ ] d) It was a member of the Frank family.

8) Why did Anne write in her diary to Kitty?
- [ ] a) She intended to give it to Kitty once she was free.
- [x] b) She needed a friend to confide in.
- [ ] c) She wanted to publish her diary.
- [ ] d) She did not want to talk to her family.

9) How did the family survive without being detected?
- [ ] a) Food was supplied to them by allies.
- [ ] b) They snuck out at night and stole food.
- [ ] c) They grew their own food.
- [x] d) They collected their rations in disguise.

10) What do you think Anne Frank's story has come to symbolise?
- [ ] a) The liberation of the concentration camps.
- [ ] b) The suffering of Jewish children during the war.
- [x] c) The consequences of a betrayal of trust.
- [ ] d) All those that died during the Second World War.

Complete the word on the right so that it means the same as, or nearly the same as, the word on the left.

11) **unattached** — d i s c o n n e c t e d

12) **genial** — f r e i n d l y

13) **creative** — a r t i s t i c

14) **credible** — t _ _ s t _ _ r t h _

15) **confront** — c h _ _ l _ n _ e

Choose the word that has a similar meaning to the words in both sets of brackets.

16) (stick, cane) (staff) baton squad pole troop
    (crew, workforce)

17) (vulgar, coarse) rude net (rough) gross brand
    (total, whole)

18) (prey, victim) (target) quarry ditch game extract
    (pit, mine)

19) (universal, widespread) magnitude (total) bulk collective mass
    (weight, size)

20) (folio, sheet) piece (servant) page leaf aide
    (attendant, bellboy)

Choose the word that means the opposite of the word on the left.

21) **hoard** squander keep collect stash

22) **honourable** moral corrupt admirable cursed

23) **impulsive** overwhelming obsessive reckless cautious

24) **ill-tempered** irritable amiable volatile irksome

25) **courteous** gallant polite rude disappointing

Score Percentage 32 %

Verbal Activity Test 11

Read the following passage carefully.

According to 12th century legend, Arthur was the illegitimate son of King Uther Pendragon and Igraine (wife of Duke Gorlois of Cornwall). Merlin the wizard placed Arthur under the care of the King's loyal ally, Sir Ector. Arthur was raised in Ector's castle in Bala (modern Wales) alongside Sir Ector's true son, Sir Kay. No one knew of Arthur's royal identity, including himself. Thinking Arthur was of a low status, Sir Kay teased and mocked him. (4)

Merlin frequently visited Arthur and after the boy had finished his duties, tutored him in many subjects. Although Arthur was slight in build and too weak to even lift a sword, Merlin taught him that knowledge was more important than sheer strength. Merlin believed that Arthur would make a fair and clever leader someday. (8)

King Uther Pendragon took ill and died leaving no heir. With no leader, England fell into a state of disorder where the nobility fought over the crown. In search of an answer, Merlin went to Westminster in London and placed an anvil on top of a large stone in which the magic sword, Excalibur, was inserted. Merlin drew the crowd's attention to the words inscribed on the blade: (12) (16)

'Whoever pulls this sword from this stone, is the rightful King of England.'

Nobles came from across the realm to try and withdraw the sword, but even the strongest were unsuccessful. Meanwhile, England fell into further decline and chaos. One day, when Arthur was fifteen, Merlin accompanied him to the sword in the stone, where a crowd had gathered. Sir Kay was present and endeavoured to remove the sword, but failed. When it was Arthur's turn he pulled it easily from the anvil. There was great rejoicing and Arthur was crowned King. (20) (24)

Notes on Text:
Illegitimate (line 1) – a child born outside of marriage

Now answer the following questions.

1) What does 'endeavoured' (line 23) mean?
   a) Gave up
   b) Failed
   c) Tried hard
   d) Succeeded

2) Where did Arthur grow up?
   - [ ] a) South-west Britain
   - [ ] b) Cornwall
   - [x] c) West Britain
   - [x] d) Westminster

3) What is an 'anvil' (line 15)?
   - [x] a) A block for shaping metal
   - [ ] b) A hammer
   - [ ] c) A big rock
   - [x] d) A sword

4) Who was Arthur's father?
   - [ ] a) Merlin
   - [ ] b) Sir Ector
   - [x] c) King Uther Pendragon
   - [ ] d) Duke Gorlois of Cornwall

5) Why did the nobles fight?
   - [x] a) They were fighting for power.
   - [ ] b) They did not like each other.
   - [x] c) They wanted to crown Sir Kay.
   - [ ] d) They claimed they were the true heirs.

6) How were Arthur and Sir Kay related?
   - [ ] a) Brothers
   - [ ] b) Stepbrothers
   - [x] c) No relation
   - [ ] d) Cousins

7) Why did Sir Kay bully Arthur?
   - [ ] a) Arthur was a badly behaved servant
   - [x] b) Sir Kay believed he was of a higher social standing
   - [x] c) Arthur wanted Sir Kay's title
   - [ ] d) Arthur was Sir Ector's favourite

8) What made Arthur a worthy king?
   - [ ] a) He was physically strong enough to withdraw the sword.
   - [ ] b) He was uneducated and of low status.
   - [x] c) He could fight well with a sword.
   - [ ] d) He was able to make wise and just decisions.

9) At what point in his life did Arthur become king?
   - [ ] a) At his birth
   - [x] b) When he was a child
   - [ ] c) When he was a teenager
   - [ ] d) As an adult

10) What kind of country had England become after King Uther Pendragon's death?
    - [x] a) In a state of civil war
    - [ ] b) Organised
    - [ ] c) Boisterous
    - [ ] d) Peaceful

Choose the correct words from the word bank to complete the passage.

A resources	B linked	C fertile	D course	E long
F disputed	G sites	H believed	I source	J water

11) __disputed__ to be the longest river in the world, the River Nile is approximately 6,650 kilometres 12) __long__. Located in north-eastern Africa, it is thought that the Nile's water 13) __sorce__ are associated with eleven countries, however the 14) __water__ of the Nile is often 15) __linked__. Although generally 16) __belived__ to Ancient

44

Egypt, only 22% of the Nile's **17)** __resources__ passes through Egypt.

Nearly all of Egypt's historical and cultural **18)** __sites__ are located along its riverbanks. Ancient Egyptians lived near the Nile as it provided

19) __fertile__, food, transportation and excellent soil for growing crops.

This is due to the **20)** __corse__ green valley created by the river across the desert.

Rearrange the words so that each sentence makes sense. Underline the word which does NOT fit into the sentence.

21) the by meeting attended staff the with entire was

22) is the prizes winning worth novel award reading

23) dictionary a hand at when too reading keep I close

24) red suddenly our train a stopped at light can

25) put take home remember the go out you please fire before to

Verbal Activity Test 12

Read the following passage carefully.

Tyrannosaurus rex was a huge, ferocious, meat-eating dinosaur that lived during the Cretaceous period. It became extinct, along with all other dinosaurs, about 65 million years ago. 'Tyrannosaurus' comes from the Greek words meaning 'tyrant lizard', while the word 'rex' means 'king' in Latin. (4) Tyrannosaurus rex is often abbreviated to T-Rex. There are more than 50 well-preserved fossils for palaeontologists to study, some of which are nearly complete skeletons. T-Rex lived in an area of the Earth which now forms Northwestern America. (8)

T-Rex walked on two legs, balancing its huge head with a long and heavy tail that contained approximately 40 spinal vertebrae. It was over 13m in length, up to 6m tall and could weigh up to seven tons. Its thick, heavy skull and 1.2-metre-long jaw enabled it to crush bones and eat nearly 230 kilograms of (12) meat in one bite. T-Rex's serrated, conical teeth were up to 30cm in length, the largest of any carnivorous dinosaur. They were used to pierce and grip flesh, which was then ripped away with its powerful neck muscles. Scientists estimate that T-Rex could run from 11mph to 43mph. (16)

Palaeontologists have debated whether T-Rex was a top predator or a scavenger. It had small but extremely powerful arms with two clawed fingers, which could have seized prey but may have struggled to hold on to it. Its arms were also too short to reach its own mouth suggesting it may have been (20) a scavenger. On the other hand, it had forward pointing eyes enabling it to judge distance, which would have made it easier for it to hunt making it an efficient predator. However, palaeontologists have now concluded that T-Rex was probably both an opportunistic predator and a scavenger. (24)

Notes on Text:
Palaeontologists (line 6) - scientists who study fossils

Now answer the following questions.

1) What does the word conical (line 13) mean?
   - [ ] a) Round and pointed
   - [ ] b) Blunt and curved
   - [x] c) Sharp and knife-like
   - [ ] d) Long and square

2) How tall was T-Rex?
   - [ ] a) The height of a bungalow
   - [ ] b) As tall as a cart horse
   - [ ] c) The height of a two storey house
   - [x] d) As high as an electric pylon

3) How many bones did T-Rex have in its back?
   - [ ] a) Less than 30
   - [ ] b) 65
   - [x] c) More than 35
   - [ ] d) 230

4) What does T-Rex most resemble?
   - [ ] a) A mammal
   - [ ] b) A reptile
   - [ ] c) A giant insect
   - [x] d) An amphibian

5) Was T-Rex more of a predator than a scavenger?
   - [ ] a) T-Rex was more of a predator
   - [ ] b) T-Rex only hunted rarely
   - [ ] c) T-Rex had more of a tendency to scavenge
   - [x] d) Scientists are undecided but it was probably both

6) What advantages did the position of T-Rex's eyes offer?
   - [ ] a) It could only spot prey at close range
   - [x] b) It had binocular vision
   - [ ] c) It could see in the dark
   - [ ] d) It had panoramic vision

7) How many digits did T-Rex have on each of its upper limbs?
   - [ ] a) One
   - [ ] b) Two
   - [x] c) Three
   - [ ] d) Four

8) How quickly could T-Rex move?
   - [ ] a) Less than 10mph
   - [ ] b) More than 50 mph
   - [ ] c) Somewhere between 10 and 45mph
   - [x] d) Over 40mph

9) Why was the Greek word 'tyrant' and the Latin word 'king' used to describe this dinosaur?
   - [ ] a) It was a very powerful and ruthless creature.
   - [ ] b) It stole prey from other dinosaurs.
   - [ ] c) It ruled all the other dinosaurs.
   - [x] d) It was the largest dinosaur that ever existed.

10) Why do we know so much about the T-Rex dinosaur?
    - [ ] a) There are cave drawings of T-Rex.
    - [ ] b) We have many footprints of the dinosaur.
    - [ ] c) It lasted longer than all the other dinosaurs.
    - [x] d) There are many preserved remains.

Choose the word that means the same as the word on the left.

11) **error** — right | skid | **blunder** ✓ | accuracy

12) **inspirational** — **encouraging** ✓ | mundane | pleasing | boring

13) **indecent** — **incorrupt** ✓ | fierce | sensible | offensive

14) **ethical** — imperial | **principled** ✓ | dishonest | proud

15) **experienced** — adequate | inept | **skilled** ✓ | amateur

Complete the word on the right so that it means the opposite of the word on the left.

16) **restrain** — r e _ e _ _ e

17) **placid** — _ x _ t _ b _ e

18) **prompt** — t _ r d _

19) **remorseful** — u n r _ p _ _ t a n _

20) **foul** — p _ e _ s _ _ t

Four of the words in each list are linked. Mark the rectangle under the word that is NOT related to these four.

21) panda   snake   bat   chimpanzee   sloth

22) pollute   contaminate   tarnish   sanitise   infect

23) twig   bough   trunk   branch   sapling

24) brash   timid   introverted   bashful   reserved

25) invoiced   juicer   misplaced   spiced   officer

Score ☐   Percentage ☐ %

Verbal Activity Test 13

Read the following passage carefully.

Alexei Nikolaevich Romanov was the only son of Tsar Nicholas II, making him the Tsarevich (heir) of the all-powerful Russian throne. Alexei was born in August 1904 in St Petersburg and was the youngest of Nicholas II's five children. As Alexei was their only son, he was incredibly precious to his parents. (4)

Alexei suffered from haemophilia, a genetic disease that prevents blood from clotting properly, meaning even a small cut or bruise was life threatening. Alexei was energetic, naughty and had to be closely watched. Andrei Derevenko, a sailor who devotedly served the Romanov's for over 10 years, was appointed to look after Alexei and carry him to prevent injuries. (8)

When he was three, Alexei cut himself while playing in the park and bled profusely. The best doctors were unable to cure him. Alexandra, his mother, was so desperate she called for the peasant faith healer, Grigori Rasputin, who prayed for Alexei and he recovered. In 1912, the juddering of a carriage ride caused a haematoma in Alexei's thigh to rupture and he received the last sacrament. Rasputin prophesied: "The little one will not die" and Alexei survived. The Russian nobility were unhappy with Rasputin's meddling in affairs of state while Russia was at war with Germany and they murdered him. (12) (16)

When Nicholas II took command of the Russian army in 1915, Alexei began to travel with him, attending meetings. The war went badly and helped spark the Revolution in 1917 which forced Nicholas II to abdicate. Eventually, the whole family was imprisoned by the Bolshevik Government. While captive, Alexei seriously injured himself by sliding down stairs on a tray. He spent his last months in a wheelchair. Sadly, the family were murdered by the Bolsheviks in July 1918. (20) (24)

Notes on Text:
Tsar (line 1) - emperor of Russia. Derived from Roman emperors called Caesar.
Haematoma (line 15) – a swelling caused by internal bleeding
Last sacrament (line 16) - a ceremony or rite for the dying
Bolsheviks (line 26) - the Russian communists

Now answer the questions on the following pages.

1) What does haemophilia cause?
    - [x] a) Bleeding that does not easily stop
    - [ ] b) Fatigue and tiredness
    - [ ] c) Certain death
    - [ ] d) Severe scarring

2) How old was Alexei when he died?
    - [ ] a) Twelve
    - [ ] b) Thirteen
    - [x] c) Fourteen
    - [ ] d) Fifteen

3) How many sisters did Alexei have?
    - [ ] a) Two
    - [ ] b) Three
    - [x] c) Four
    - [ ] d) Five

4) Why was Rasputin so important to Alexandra?
    - [ ] a) He was an important advisor to Nicholas II.
    - [ ] b) Rasputin administered the last rites to Alexei.
    - [x] c) Everything Rasputin said always came true.
    - [x] d) She believed that Rasputin had healing powers.

5) What kind of child was Alexei?
    - [ ] a) Calm and well behaved
    - [x] b) Active and mischievous
    - [ ] c) Shy and timid
    - [ ] d) Noisy and boisterous

6) How did his parents keep Alexei safe?
    - [x] a) A personal minder took care of him.
    - [ ] b) Alexei was not allowed to go outside.
    - [ ] c) There was always a doctor at hand.
    - [ ] d) He was forbidden to play like other children.

7) Why was Alexei so important for the future of Russia?
   - a) He was treasured by his parents and the Russian people.
   - b) If his illness was cured it would benefit other Russians.
   - [x] c) He assisted his father in military decisions during World War I.
   - d) One day he would rule Russia.

8) What caused Alexei to be unable to walk?
   - a) A bumpy journey in a carriage.
   - b) Tripping over in the park.
   - [x] c) An accident on some steps.
   - d) Being dropped unintentionally by Derevenko.

9) What was responsible for the demise of the Romanovs?
   - a) The communist party
   - b) World War I
   - [x] c) Rasputin's murder
   - d) The Russian Revolution

10) How well do you think Alexei coped while being held captive?
    - a) He became depressed and reclusive
    - b) He refused to do anything and had to be assisted at all times
    - c) He remained cheerful and upbeat
    - [x] d) He behaved cautiously because he was being watched

Select the correct words to complete the passage.

Piranhas are fish with a ferocious 11) [rank / **impression** / reputation] that 12) [**inhabit** / inhibit / inherit] the rivers of South America. Approximately 20 species of piranha are 13) [acquired / found / **obtained**] in the Amazon River. Piranhas are normally 14-26cm long, although some 14) ☐ specialisms / ☐ spectrums / ☑ specimens can be up to 43cm. All piranhas have rows of

sharp teeth which are used for rapid puncture and 15) ☐ shearling / ☑ shearing / ☐ sheathing. Despite the

common 16) ☑ certainty / ☐ belief / ☐ confidence that they are blood-thirsty, most piranha species are

actually quite harmless and 17) ☑ docile / ☐ feral / ☐ toxic. They are omnivorous animals

meaning they eat both animals and plants. The 18) ☐ bread / ☐ braid / ☑ breed notorious for

aggressive behaviour are the red-bellied piranha. Their silver bodies are covered

with red patches to 19) ☑ camouflage / ☐ concealment / ☐ reveal them in 20) ☐ slimy / ☑ muddy / ☐ filth waters.

Complete the word on the right so that it means the same as, or nearly the same as, the word on the left.

21) **outrageous** d i s g r a c e f u l   *disgraceful.*

22) **uncouth** v u l g a r ✗

23) **mammoth** e n o r m o u s ✓

24) **sensible** p r a c t i c a l ✗

25) **deft** s k i l f u l ✗

Verbal Activity Test 14

> Read the following passage carefully.

In the ancient kingdom of England there existed a hillock in the middle of a dense forest. On their return from battle, the knights often rested there against a great oak tree, because they were tired and thirsty. However there was no stream or brook in the woods. (4)

One of the King's favourite knights, Baldwin, was so parched he called out, "I thirst!"
Immediately from the shadows a strange, goblin-like creature appeared. He was dressed in a beautiful crimson robe and smiled at Baldwin. In his (8) *outstretched hand he held a large drinking-vessel that was richly ornamented with gold and precious jewels and contained an unknown beverage.*

Baldwin drank from the goblet and found the delicious drink refreshed and cooled him. The goblin then offered Baldwin a silk napkin to wipe his (12) *mouth. Then, without waiting to be thanked, the strange creature vanished as suddenly as he had come.*

A year later, a knight called Madoc with a coarse and rude nature, was hunting alone in the forest. After failing to catch anything he sat down, (16) *exhausted by the great oak tree.*
Feeling thirsty, he cried out, "I thirst!"
Instantly the goblin emerged and presented the drinking vessel to Madoc. The knight drained the beverage in one gulp, but instead of returning the vessel, he (20) *clutched it to his chest and rode away at great speed.*

Madoc boasted far and wide of his deed, but when Baldwin heard of it he had Madoc bound and cast into prison. Fearing he might be accused of partaking in the theft and the ingratitude of the knight, Baldwin presented the jewelled (24) *vessel to the King. It was carefully preserved and stored among the royal treasures, but the benevolent goblin was never seen again.*

An adapted extract from the story 'The Benevolent Goblin' from the medieval anthology *Gesta Romanorum*.

> Now answer the following questions.

1) What do you think 'benevolent' (line 26) means?
   - [x] a) Malicious
   - [ ] b) Grovelling
   - [ ] c) Generous
   - [ ] d) Demanding

2) How was the creature dressed?
- [ ] a) In an orange robe
- [x] b) In a red gown ✗
- [ ] c) In a brown coat
- [ ] d) In a purple cloak

3) What word is used for a drink?
- [x] a) Beverage ✓
- [ ] b) Vessel
- [ ] c) Gulp
- [ ] d) Goblet

4) What does Baldwin's behaviour teach us?
- [x] a) To be just and grateful
- [ ] b) To be selfish and unthankful
- [ ] c) To be cruel and greedy
- [x] d) To be vengeful and kingly ✗

5) What had to be done in order for the goblin to appear?
- [ ] a) Suffer from thirst
- [ ] b) Call for the creature
- [ ] c) Sit under the oak tree
- [x] d) Call out, "I thirst!" ✓

6) Why was Madoc punished?
- [ ] a) He did not feel guilty
- [x] b) He stole the goblin's cup ✓
- [ ] c) He was coarse and rude
- [ ] d) He was ungrateful

7) What did the goblin require in return for his kindness?
- [ ] a) Thanks
- [ ] b) A reward
- [ ] c) Royal approval ✓
- [x] d) Nothing

8) Where did the goblin reside?
    - [ ] a) By a brook
    - [x] b) In an oak tree
    - [ ] c) On a small hill
    - [ ] d) On the edge of a forest

9) What happened to the goblet?
    - [x] a) It was kept in the royal treasury
    - [x] ~~b) Baldwin returned it to the goblin~~
    - [ ] c) It disappeared
    - [x] ~~d) Madoc kept it~~

10) What quality did both knights exhibit by taking an 'unknown beverage' (line 10) from the goblin?
    - [ ] a) Disregard
    - [x] b) Trust
    - [ ] c) Suspicion
    - [ ] d) Gluttony

Choose the word that has a similar meaning to the words in both sets of brackets.

11) (exceed, surpass) (summit, peak)
    beat   top   conference   outdo   (highest)

12) (stone, seed) (ditch, trench)
    gutter   kernel   channel   (pit)   pebble

13) (texture, surface) (granule, particle)
    grain   (speck)   quality   pellet   morsel

14) (isolate, quarantine) (emblem, insignia)
    separate   (symbol)   seal   seclusion   sign

15) (contest, game) (replica, equivalent)
    model   race   alike   gala   (match)

Choose the word that means the opposite of the word on the left.

16)	**diminutive**	minute ☐	thorough ☐	petite ☐	huge ☑
17)	**vulgar**	tasteful ☑	cheap ☐	rough ☐	wilful ☐
18)	**kindle**	ignite ☐	read ☐	douse ☑	race ☐
19)	**humane**	creature ☐	kind ☐	person ☐	cruel ☑
20)	**knowledgeable**	erudite ☑	ignorant ☐	educated ☐	inconsiderate ✗

Complete the word on the right so that it means the same as, or nearly the same as, the word on the left.

21) **villainous** — w i c k e d

22) **tolerant** — _ c _ e _ t i n g

23) **deferential** — r e s p e c t f u l

24) **outrun** — s u r p a s s

25) **jocular** — h u m e r o u s

Score ☐ Percentage ☐ %

Verbal Activity Test 15

Read the following passage carefully.

Mowgli, a boy, was lost in the jungle and raised by wolves. He is eleven years old.

Father Wolf taught him his business, and the meaning of things in the jungle, till every rustle in the grass, every breath of the warm night air, every note of the owls above his head, every scratch of a bat's claws as it roosted in a tree, and every splash of every little fish jumping in a pool meant just as much to (4) him as office work means to a business man. When he was not learning he sat out in the sun and slept, and ate and went to sleep again.

When he felt dirty or hot he swam in the forest pools; and when he wanted honey, Baloo the bear told him that honey and nuts were just as pleasant to (8) eat as raw meat. Bagheera the black panther showed him how to climb up for them.

Bagheera would lay on a branch and call, "Come along, Little Brother." At first Mowgli would cling like the sloth, but afterward he would fling himself (12) through the branches almost as boldly as the grey ape.

He took his place, too, at the Council Rock when the Pack met, and there he discovered that if he stared hard at any wolf, the wolf would be forced to drop his eyes, and so he used to stare for fun. At other times he would pick the long (16) thorns out of the pads of his friends, for wolves suffer terribly from thorns and burs in their coats.

He would go down the hillside into the cultivated lands by night, and look curiously at the villagers in their huts. He mistrusted men because Bagheera (20) showed him a trap cunningly hidden in the jungle.

An adapted extract from *The Jungle Book* by Rudyard Kipling (1865-1936).

<u>Notes on Text:</u>
Council Rock (line 14) – the meeting place of the wolves
Mowgli – means 'the frog'. The wolves gave him this name because he had no fur and was unable to stay still.

Now answer the following questions.

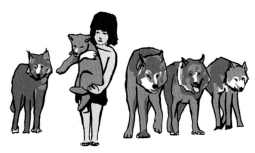

1) Where did the wolves meet?
   - [ ] a) By the forest pools
   - [ ] b) The hillside
   - [x] c) The Council Rock
   - [ ] d) Near the village

2) Who taught Mowgli how to climb trees?
- [ ] a) Baloo
- [x] b) Bagheera
- [ ] c) Father Wolf
- [ ] d) The grey ape

3) What kind of boy was Mowgli?
- [x] a) Playful, inquisitive and caring
- [ ] b) Lazy, sleepy and always hungry
- [ ] c) Greedy, selfish and boisterous
- [ ] d) Mischievous, cunning and badly behaved

4) How did Mowgli feel about his own kind?
- [x] a) He wanted to live with them.
- [ ] b) He disliked their way of life.
- [x] c) He wanted nothing to do with them.
- [ ] d) He was wary of them.

5) How are wolf and human behaviour similar?
- [ ] a) Wolves care for their young, eat honey and nuts and live in a pack.
- [ ] b) Wolves are meat-eaters who always hunt for their food.
- [ ] c) Wolves are lone creatures that are feared by all other animals.
- [x] d) Wolves take care of each other, dwell in family groups and teach their young.

6) What sense did Father Wolf teach Mowgli to use most?
- [ ] a) Smell
- [x] b) Sight
- [ ] c) Hearing
- [ ] d) Taste

7) What was Mowgli warned about?
- [ ] a) Falling from the trees
- [ ] b) Not to stare at wolves
- [x] c) A concealed trap
- [ ] d) Not to eat raw meat

8) What does 'cultivated' (line 19) mean?
   - [x] a) Land prepared for crops
   - [ ] b) Grazing land
   - [ ] c) Forest land
   - [ ] d) Deforested land

9) What other name did Mowgli have?
   - [ ] a) Ape Boy
   - [ ] b) Baby Wolf
   - [x] c) Little Frog
   - [ ] d) Little Brother

10) What activity amused Mowgli?
    - [ ] a) Listening to bats clawing the trees
    - [ ] b) Staring at a wolf until he looked away
    - [x] c) Climbing trees for honey
    - [ ] d) Watching the villagers

Fill in the missing letters to complete the passage.

The 11) **_n c _ _ n t** Hindu festival of Diwali (festival of lights) is celebrated 12) **worldwide** over five days in October and November every year. The festival spiritually 13) **s _ g _ i f _ e s** the victory of light over 14) **_ a r _ n _ s s**. Before Diwali night, people clean and 15) **decorate** their homes.

On Diwali night, Hindus dress up, light diyas (lamps and candles) and 16) **participate** in family prayers, typically to Lakshmi – the goddess of wealth and 17) **p _ o p _ r _ t y** - to bring them good luck in the **18)** [ ][o][ ][i][n][ ] year. After this, fireworks follow,

then a family feast and an **19)** [e][ ][ ][h][ ][ ][g][e] of gifts. Lights are left

20) [d][u][r][e][i][n][g] all night, so that Lakshmi may feel welcomed.

Rearrange the words so that each sentence makes sense. Underline the word which does NOT fit into the sentence.

21) goods must airport restricted you at for declare the

22) taste around fashion the her was latest not to

23) did diary he a to his daily resolution write made in

24) paint colour they could kitchen where the which to decide not

25) served on Day when traditionally is turkey Christmas

Score [ ] Percentage [ ]%

Verbal Activity Test 16

Read the following passage carefully.

Francis Drake was born in 1542 in Devon and went to sea aged 12. He became an English sea captain, privateer, navigator and eventually vice admiral. For most of Drake's life, Queen Elizabeth I ruled England. Under her reign the country grew in population, power and wealth, developing new trading (4) opportunities for English produce throughout the colonies.

Drake was the first Englishman to circumnavigate the world in a single expedition from 1577 to 1580, and was leader of the expedition throughout. 164 seamen departed in five ships from Plymouth, with Drake himself sailing (8) in the Pelican. On arrival in America, Drake was concerned that his ships might become separated, so he ordered two of them to be scuttled. Then the Marigold was lost and the Elizabeth returned home. By late 1578, only 58 men remained, all on the Pelican, which Drake renamed the Golden Hind. (12)

On his way back from the South American colonies, Drake plundered Spanish ships and Portuguese ports for silver, gold and spices. He kept some of the treasure and gifted the rest to the Queen. Upon his arrival home, Queen Elizabeth dined on board the Golden Hind at Deptford, on the River Thames, (16) and later knighted him. Drake's expedition improved knowledge of the world's geography.

Drake was a hero to the English but was considered a pirate by King Philip II of Spain, who offered a reward of 20,000 ducats (a ducat is worth £200 today) (20) for his life. As an enemy of Spain, Drake played a part in defeating the Spanish Armada in 1588. He was second-in-command of the English fleet and captured the Spanish flagship Rosario.

Drake died of dysentery at the age of 54 off the coast of Panama and his body (24) was buried at sea.

Notes on Text:
Scuttled (line 10) – sink one's own ship deliberately
Dysentery (line 24) – infection of the intestines

Now answer the following questions.

1) How many ships returned home from the expedition?
   - a) One
   - b) Two
   - c) Four
   - d) Five

2) What was the original name of Drake's ship?
   - [ ] a) The Golden Hind
   - [ ] b) The Elizabeth
   - [ ] c) The Marigold
   - [x] d) The Pelican

3) How many men did not complete the circumnavigation?
   - [ ] a) 54 men
   - [ ] b) 58 men
   - [x] c) 106 men
   - [ ] d) 164 men

4) What was Drake's new title upon receiving his knighthood?
   - [ ] a) Count Francis Drake
   - [x] b) Sir Francis Drake
   - [ ] c) Lord Francis Drake
   - [ ] d) Viscount Francis Drake

5) In what year did Drake die?
   - [ ] a) 1595
   - [x] b) 1596
   - [ ] c) 1597
   - [ ] d) 1598

6) How did Spain view Drake?
   - [ ] a) As a brave seaman
   - [ ] b) As a worthy opponent
   - [x] c) As a buccaneer
   - [ ] d) As a great navigator

7) What rank was vice admiral?
   - [ ] a) He was deputy commander
   - [ ] b) He was assistant privateer
   - [ ] c) He was captain of the fleet
   - [ ] d) He was chief navigator

8) Why was the capture of the Rosario so important?
   - [x] a) It contained Spanish gold.
   - [ ] b) It held the commander of the fleet.
   - [ ] c) Philip II of Spain was on-board.
   - [ ] d) It held the flag of the Spanish fleet.

9) What is Drake's lasting legacy to the world?
   - [ ] a) He made Britain very wealthy.
   - [ ] b) He defeated the Spanish.
   - [ ] c) He founded many colonies.
   - [x] d) He expanded our understanding of the globe.

10) How much would Drake's capture have been worth in pound sterling today?
    - [ ] a) Two thousand pounds
    - [ ] b) Forty thousand pounds
    - [ ] c) Two million pounds
    - [x] d) Four million pounds

Complete the word on the right so that it means the opposite of the word on the left.

11) **reverent** — d i s r e s p e c t f u l

12) **successful** — f a i l e d

13) **forgiving** — m e r c i l e s s

14) **loving** — l _ _ t h i n g *loathing*

15) **resilient** — w e a k

Four of the words in each list are linked. Mark the rectangle under the word that is NOT related to these four.

16) revealing [■]   hideous [ ]   repulsive [ ]   ugly [ ]   revolting [ ]

17) feline [ ]   sly [ ]   tom [ ]   tabby [ ]   kitten [■]

18) because [ ]   since [ ]   any [■]   unless [ ]   whether [ ]

19) straw [ ]   nametag [ ]   smart [ ]   evil [ ]   storm [ ]

20) dash [ ]   ellipsis [ ]   smudge [■]   hyphen [ ]   point [ ]

Choose the word that means the same as the word on the left.

21) **vulnerable**   defenceless [■]   invincible [ ]   severe [ ]   miserable [ ]

22) **marine**   nausea [ ]   naughty [ ]   nautical [■]   naught [ ]

23) **upstanding**   weak [ ]   attitude [ ]   shelf [ ]   vertical [■]

24) **attentive**   accusing [ ]   observant [■]   signal [ ]   careless [ ]

25) **integrity**   ability [ ]   deceit [ ]   honesty [ ]   tranquillity [ ]

Score 18/25   Percentage 72 %

Verbal Activity Test 17

> Read the following passage carefully.

Two Little Kittens

Two little kittens, one stormy night,
Began to quarrel, and then to fight;
One had a mouse, the other had none,
And that's the way the quarrel begun. (4)

"I'll have that mouse," said the biggest cat;
"You'll have that mouse? We'll see about that!"
"I will have that mouse," said the eldest son;
"You shan't have the mouse," said the little one. (8)

I told you before 'twas a stormy night
When these two little kittens began to fight;
The old woman seized her sweeping broom,
And swept the two kittens right out of the room. (12)

The ground was covered with frost and snow,
And the two little kittens had nowhere to go;
So they laid them down on the mat at the door,
While the old woman finished sweeping the floor. (16)

Then they crept in, as quiet as mice,
All wet with the snow, and cold as ice,
For they found it was better, that stormy night,
To lie down and sleep than to quarrel and fight. (20)

By Anonymous (circa 1880).

> Now answer the following questions.

1) What is the rhyming pattern of this poem?
   - ☐ a) Alternate lines in each stanza rhyme or ABAB.
   - ☐ b) The first and third lines of each stanza rhyme or ABAC.
   - ☐ c) Each stanza is in rhyming couplets or AABB.
   - ☐ d) The second and fourth lines of each stanza rhyme or ABCB.

2) How many similes are there in this poem?
- [ ] a) None
- [ ] b) One
- [ ] c) Two
- [ ] d) Three

3) What is the moral of this poem?
- [ ] a) If you are first to claim something it belongs to you.
- [ ] b) It is better to share things rather than fight over them.
- [ ] c) If you fight then fight to win.
- [ ] d) Always be prepared to give away your possessions.

4) What kind of poem is this?
- [ ] a) Narrative poem
- [ ] b) A ballad
- [ ] c) Lyric poem
- [ ] d) A limerick

5) In which stanza do all the lines have the same number of beats?
- [ ] a) First
- [ ] b) Second
- [ ] c) Third
- [ ] d) Fifth

6) What was the weather like?
- [ ] a) It was cold and snowy.
- [ ] b) It was sunny and warm.
- [ ] c) It was wet and windy.
- [ ] d) It was calm and dry.

7) What poetic technique is used in the second stanza?
- [ ] a) Alliteration
- [ ] b) Onomatopoeia
- [ ] c) Anaphora
- [ ] d) Hyperbole

8) How does line 9 end?
- [ ] a) With a semi-colon
- [ ] b) With a caesura
- [ ] c) With a comma
- [ ] d) With an enjambment

9) How did the kittens end up outside?
- [ ] a) They ran outside.
- [ ] b) They were brushed out.
- [ ] c) They chased the mouse outside.
- [ ] d) They were thrown out.

10) Why did the kittens fight?
- [ ] a) They both wanted the mouse.
- [ ] b) The older kitten liked to bully the younger kitten.
- [ ] c) The old woman gave them a mouse to share.
- [ ] d) The kittens hated each other.

Choose the correct words from the word bank to complete the passage.

A spread	B standard	C patented	D designers	E invented
F concert	G inventor	H poverty	I reputation	J teaching

Antoine-Joseph "Adolphe" Sax (1814-1894) was a Belgian 11) _____

and musician who played the flute and clarinet. His parents were instrument

12) _____ and Adolphe began to make his own instruments at an early

age. His instruments 13) _____ rapidly. Around 1840 he developed the

instrument for which he is best known, the saxophone, 14) _____ on

28 June 1846. The saxophone was 15) _____ for use in both orchestras

and **16)** _____ bands. Although they never became **17)** _____ orchestral instruments, the saxophones made his **18)** _____ and secured him a job, **19)** _____ at the Paris Conservatoire in 1857. In 1894 Sax died in complete **20)** _____ in Paris.

Rearrange the words so that each sentence makes sense. Underline the word which does NOT fit into the sentence.

21) enough back vote not was he yet old to

22) trade such she of the him the tricks taught

23) the opening the mayor attended ceremony were historic

24) none to wet not on be the slip floor careful

25) route will time journey take you the take down same whichever the

Score [ ] Percentage [ ] %

Verbal Activity Test 18

Read the following passage carefully.

Shirley Temple (1928-2014) was a curly-haired American film actress, singer and dancer, most famous as Hollywood's number-one box-office star from 1935 through 1938.

Shirley began dancing at three years old. In 1932 some producers, who were (4) making a series of short films, spotted her. These were parodies of famous films with all-child casts. As the star, Shirley was paid $10 a day. She then landed a role in Fox Corporation's 1933 film, *Stand Up and Cheer*, where her dancing and acting ability amazed everybody. (8)

In 1934, the feature film *Bright Eyes* was specifically written for her. She was the youngest star ever to receive a Juvenile Oscar in 1935 from the Academy for her outstanding contribution to motion pictures. Other hits such as *Curly Top* and *Heidi* soon followed, gaining her international fame and leading to (12) the sale of merchandise, including dolls and clothing. However, her popularity waned as she reached adolescence. She appeared in *The Blue Bird* in 1940, which was unsuccessful at the box office. At age 19, she co-starred in *The Bachelor and the Bobby Soxer*, but audiences found it difficult to accept (16) that Shirley was growing up. Shirley retired completely from films in 1950, although she appeared on television periodically.

Temple received the Screen Actors Guild Life Achievement Award in 2005. She is ranked 18th on the list of greatest female American screen legends. She (20) once joked that the key to her success was that she was born at 9 o'clock in the evening and was "Too late for dinner [...], started life one meal behind [and] ever since [had] tried to make up for that loss."

Shirley starred in 14 short films, 43 feature films and over 25 children's TV (24) films from 1932 until 1961.

Notes on Text:
Parodies (line 5) – comic versions of well-known plays or films

Now answer the following questions.

1) How many decades did Shirley Temple's career span?
   - a) Half a decade
   - b) One decade
   - c) Two decades
   - d) Three decades

2) Which was the first film commissioned especially for Shirley to star in?
   - ☐ a) *Stand Up and Cheer*
   - ☐ b) *Bright Eyes*
   - ☐ c) *Curly Top*
   - ☐ d) *The Bachelor and the Bobby Soxer*

3) What award did Shirley receive when she was six years old?
   - ☐ a) An Academy Award
   - ☐ b) Fox Corporation's Award
   - ☐ c) Life Achievement Award
   - ☐ d) Hollywood Child Star Award

4) What did Shirley Temple attribute her own success to?
   - ☐ a) Hard work
   - ☐ b) Luck
   - ☐ c) Talent
   - ☐ d) She could sing, dance and act

5) Why do you think Shirley became less popular in her teens?
   - ☐ a) She was not a good adolescent actress.
   - ☐ b) Other child stars took her place.
   - ☐ c) Audiences loved her child persona.
   - ☐ d) She was not offered good roles.

6) How did Shirley's career begin?
   - ☐ a) With the feature film *Bright Eyes*
   - ☐ b) With her starring role in a stage musical
   - ☐ c) With humorous spoof movies
   - ☐ d) With her introduction to dance lessons

7) What was the most successful period of Shirley's career?
   - ☐ a) 1932-1942
   - ☐ b) The early 1930s
   - ☐ c) 1940s
   - ☐ d) 1935-1938

8) What resulted from Shirley Temple's popularity?
- [ ] a) An increase in children's dance lessons
- [ ] b) Many branded products
- [ ] c) Awards named after her
- [ ] d) Other child stars imitating her

9) What film was specifically named after Shirley's appearance?
- [ ] a) *Curly Top*
- [ ] b) *The Bachelor and the Bobby Soxer*
- [ ] c) *The Blue Bird*
- [ ] d) *Heidi*

10) How many films did Shirley appear in?
- [ ] a) 43
- [ ] b) Nearly 60
- [ ] c) Almost 70
- [ ] d) Over 80

Choose the word that means the same as the word on the left.

11) **waspish**	cordial	irritable	dangerous	secure
12) **lethargy**	weariness	vigour	fragility	power
13) **keen**	cool	impassive	eager	whole
14) **apathetic**	excited	indifferent	loose	difficult
15) **zany**	subdued	devoted	tepid	eccentric

Complete the word on the right so that it means the same as, or nearly the same as, the word on the left.

16) **trustworthy**   d _ p e _ d _ b _ e

17) **simple**   _ t r a _ g h t _ o r _ a r _

18) **confine**   _ n c l _ s _

19) **perceptive**   i n _ i g _ t _ u _

20) **exquisite**   b _ _ _ t _ f u l

Choose the word that has a similar meaning to the words in both sets of brackets.

21) (incubate, brood)   raise   invent   rear   plan   hatch
     (devise, concoct)

22) (mark, stroke)   punch   whip   tick   snap   hit
     (click, clack)

23) (beaker, cup)   mug   raid   glass   tumbler   pint
     (assault, rob)

24) (student, schoolchild)   see   scholar   orb   pupil   student
     (iris, eye)

25) (remainder, residue)   salon   rest   excess   recline   balance
     (lounge, relax)

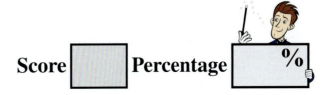

Verbal Activity Test 19

> Read the following passage carefully.

The Fieldmouse

Where the acorn tumbles down,
Where the ash tree sheds its berry,
With your fur so soft and brown,
With your eye so round and merry, (4)
Scarcely moving the long grass,
Fieldmouse, I can see you pass.

Little thing, in what dark den,
Lie you all the winter sleeping? (8)
Till warm weather comes again,
Then once more I see you peeping
Round about the tall tree roots,
Nibbling at their fallen fruits. (12)

Fieldmouse, fieldmouse, do not go,
Where the farmer stacks his treasure,
Find the nut that falls below,
Eat the acorn at your pleasure, (16)
But you must not steal the grain
He has stacked with so much pain.

Make your hole where mosses spring,
Underneath the tall oak's shadow, (20)
Pretty, quiet harmless thing,
Play about the sunny meadow.
Keep away from corn and house,
None will harm you, little mouse. (24)

By Cecil Frances Alexander (1818-1895).

> Now answer the following questions.

1) Where does the fieldmouse live?
   - [ ] a) An underground nest below the trees.
   - [ ] b) In the branches of an oak tree.
   - [ ] c) In the haystacks.
   - [ ] d) In the long grass.

2) Which of the following does the fieldmouse eat in the poem?
- [ ] a) Worms, fruit and grain
- [ ] b) Nuts, grain and centipedes
- [ ] c) Grain, fruit and nuts
- [ ] d) Fruit, fungi and grain

3) Why do farmers dislike the fieldmouse?
- [ ] a) They make holes in sacks.
- [ ] b) They eat the grain.
- [ ] c) They scare the farmers' wives.
- [ ] d) They eat acorns.

4) The use of 'warm weather' and 'fallen fruit' are examples of what?
- [ ] a) Assonance
- [ ] b) Onomatopoeia
- [ ] c) Consonance
- [ ] d) Alliteration

5) What does the fieldmouse sometimes do in cold weather?
- [ ] a) Build a new nest.
- [ ] b) Hibernate.
- [ ] c) Move to the farmhouse.
- [ ] d) Eat more food than usual.

6) What form of verse is this poem?
- [ ] a) Formal verse
- [ ] b) Prose
- [ ] c) Free verse
- [ ] d) Haiku

7) How does the fieldmouse obtain its food?
- [ ] a) It hunts.
- [ ] b) It forages.
- [ ] c) It climbs trees.
- [ ] d) It steals it from other animals.

8) How do some people mentioned in this poem view the fieldmouse?
- [ ] a) As a pest
- [ ] b) As a food source
- [ ] c) As a pet
- [ ] d) As dangerous creature

9) What kind of character is the fieldmouse?
- [ ] a) It is an aggressive, powerful creature.
- [ ] b) It is lazy, greedy creature.
- [ ] c) It is a busy, devious creature.
- [ ] d) It is a gentle, peaceful creature.

10) Why is the word 'fieldmouse' repeated in line 13?
- [ ] a) The fieldmouse is the subject of the poem.
- [ ] b) There is more than one fieldmouse.
- [ ] c) The narrator is giving the rodent a warning.
- [ ] d) The narrator is telling the fieldmouse it can be seen.

Select the correct words to complete the passage.

Mayday is the word used 11) [ ] internally / [ ] intellectually / [ ] internationally as a distress call in radio 12) [ ] communications / [ ] transcriptions / [ ] plays. The use of the word 13) [ ] gestures / [ ] signals / [ ] cries a life-threatening emergency, usually on a ship or a plane. 14) [ ] Law / [ ] Protocol / [ ] Politeness dictates that the call is always said three times in a row, 'Mayday! Mayday! Mayday!' to 15) [ ] prevent / [ ] permit / [ ] faction mistaking it for another word or phrase under 16) [ ] stressed / [ ] hoarse / [ ] noisy conditions. The word was **17)** ☐ convinced / ☐ conflicted / ☐ conceived by Frederick Stanley Mockford, a

senior radio officer at Croydon Airport, London. It **18)** ☐ originates / ☐ deviates / ☐ permeates from the

French 'm'aidez' meaning 'help me'. In the United States it is illegal to make a

19) ☐ fiction / ☐ false / ☐ copy distress call carrying a **20)** ☐ penalty / ☐ fee / ☐ penalise of up to six years

imprisonment or a $250,000 fine.

Complete the word on the right so that it means the opposite of the word on the left.

21) **hostile**   _ r _ _ n d l y

22) **honest**   d e c _ _ t f u _

23) **qualify**   _ a i _

24) **grouchy**   c _ e _ r _ u _

25) **contract**   _ x p _ n _

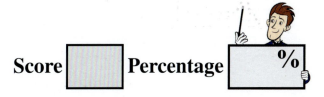

Verbal Activity Test 20

Read the following passage carefully.

The Beverley children were orphaned during the English Civil War (1642-1649) when the Roundheads had rebelled against King Charles I. The children hid from the Roundheads in the New Forest and learnt to fend for themselves. Here, twelve-year-old Humphrey rescues a gypsy boy called Pablo from a trap.

It was the end of March, and the weather was mild. Humphrey arrived at the pit, and it was sufficiently light for him to perceive that the covering had been broken in, and therefore something must have been trapped. He sat down and waited for daylight. At times he thought he heard heavy breathing, and once a (4) low groan. This made him more anxious, and he again peered into the pit, but could not discover anything, until at last he made out a human figure lying at the bottom.

    Humphrey called, "Is there anyone there?" (8)
There was a groan, and Humphrey was horrified at the idea that somebody had fallen into the pit and was injured. He recollected that the rough ladder which he had made to take the soil up out of the pit was against an oak-tree. He ran for it, put it down the pit and cautiously descended. Upon arrival at (12) the bottom, he found a half-clothed lad lying there. Humphrey turned him over, as the boy was lying face down, and shook him to ascertain whether he was alive. The lad groaned several times, and opened his eyes. Humphrey was afraid he was not strong enough to lift the boy on his shoulders and carry him (16) up the ladder. He tried and discovered due to starvation the poor lad was light enough to be lugged to the surface where Humphrey safely landed him by the side of the pit.

An adapted extract from *The Children of the New Forest* by Frederick Marryat (1792-1848).

Notes on Text:
Roundheads – were the troops of Oliver Cromwell who wore round helmets

Now answer the following questions.

1) At what time of day did Humphrey arrive at the trap?
   - [ ] a) At night
   - [ ] b) At daybreak
   - [ ] c) At dusk
   - [ ] d) At midday

2) Why did Humphrey build a trap?
- [ ] a) To catch animals for food
- [ ] b) To trap Roundheads
- [ ] c) To play tricks on his sisters
- [ ] d) To store foraged food

3) What was unusual about the weather?
- [ ] a) It was colder than expected for that month.
- [ ] b) It had not stopped raining for weeks.
- [ ] c) It was warmer than usual for that time of year.
- [ ] d) It was like summer.

4) Why was Humphrey able to lift the boy up from the trap?
- [ ] a) Humphrey was very strong.
- [ ] b) The boy help Humphrey climb up.
- [ ] c) The trap was not very deep.
- [ ] d) The boy was very thin.

5) What do you think is meant by a civil war?
- [ ] a) A war between two countries.
- [ ] b) A war between citizens of the same country.
- [ ] c) A worldwide war.
- [ ] d) A war that a King loses.

6) How did Humphrey first know that the trap held something?
- [ ] a) He could just see that the top had been disturbed.
- [ ] b) Humphrey could hear breathing.
- [ ] c) He could see something lying at the bottom.
- [ ] d) Humphrey heard a groan.

7) Why was there a ladder to hand?
- [ ] a) He had planned to use it to check the trap.
- [ ] b) He had made it to extract earth from the hole.
- [ ] c) The children had left it in the forest after picking fruit.
- [ ] d) He had made it to climb trees to be a lookout.

8) Whose side were the children on in the war?
- [ ] a) King Charles I
- [ ] b) The Roundheads
- [ ] c) Oliver Cromwell
- [ ] d) The English

9) Why was Humphrey so upset in line 9?
- [ ] a) He had not caught an animal.
- [ ] b) He was worried he had caused a person to be hurt.
- [ ] c) He would have to reset the trap.
- [ ] d) It would delay his return home.

10) Why did the children run away to the New Forest?
- [ ] a) The Roundheads had burnt their house down.
- [ ] b) They wanted an adventure and learn survival skills.
- [ ] c) They had no parents to look after them.
- [ ] d) They wanted to help children like Pablo who had no home.

Choose the word that means the opposite of the word on the left.

11)	**enthusiastic**	excited	disturbed	apathetic	thrilled
12)	**conscientious**	careless	careful	carefree	carer
13)	**indigenous**	native	foreign	local	excavate
14)	**smart**	scruffy	clever	neat	sting
15)	**celestial**	spiritual	cosmic	solar	earthly

Choose the word that has a similar meaning to the words in both sets of brackets.

16) (hobby, pastime)　　　pursuit　fad　interest　leisure　incomes
　　(profits, returns)

17) (stream, spray)　　　river　jet　inky　spritz　raven
　　(black, ebony)

18) (stop, halt)　　　source　devise　spring　close　stem
　　(derive, originate)

19) (banner, ensign)　　　flag　specify　badge　detect　emblem
　　(identify, indicate)

20) (stopper, cork)　　　hollow　cap　bung　plug　vent
　　(socket, outlet)

Choose the word that means the same as the word on the left.

21) **communicative**　　liberated　　subtle　　outgoing　　withdrawn

22) **covetous**　　persuasive　　envious　　sorceress　　generous

23) **evade**　　confront　　observe　　confuse　　avoid

24) **contrast**　　compare　　disagree　　permit　　decide

25) **fallow**　　farmed　　gulp　　unsown　　narrow

Score ☐　Percentage ☐ %

Notes

PROGRESS CHARTS

Test	Mark	%
1		
2		
3		
4		
5		
6		
7		
8		
9		
10		
11		
12		
13		
14		
15		
16		
17		
18		
19		
20		

© 2015 Stephen Curran

CERTIFICATE OF
ACHIEVEMENT

This certifies

_____

has successfully completed

11+ Verbal Activity
Year 5–7 CEM Style
TESTBOOK 1

Overall percentage score achieved [ ] %

Comment _____

_____

Signed _____
(teacher/parent/guardian)

Date _____